The Vaccine That Never Was

By
F.W. Shannon

I'm not a conspiracy theorist.

As a matter of fact, I'm not generally a fan of them.

They tend to take mole hills and make them into mountains with no credible foundation and *that* detracts from the truth. It clutters up a world of information that is already confusing enough.

This ... Is no conspiracy theory.

This is my personal account, based on my personal experience and the facts that accompany that experience.

I 'retired' from my career in the world of science in January of this year and left behind Long Island and my position with a very well-known government laboratory. The reasons for my having done so will become evident to the reader as this book unfolds ...

It was about 1 pm when the phone on my desk in my office at the lab rang.

It was March 21st, 2020.

It was the director of my department. No names … I don't need to spend the next few years in court, so there will be no names in this book. The stack of non-disclosure documents in my government file is tall enough to stand on to change a lightbulb in a ceiling fixture, so I'm going to be very careful how I word things.

I'm autistic.

Not in 'the bad way' where one is non-verbal and lives in a state of eternal detachment from the rest of the world. I think it's just a side effect of the 174 IQ.

Yah … It's that high. And it has served me well over the years to put food on the table and keep the bills paid. It landed me a pair of doctorate degrees from Columbia University and the job at the lab, so it evens out the curse I believed it to be in my youth.

But I digress.

You'll find I do that a lot.

The director of my department at the lab was in his office just one floor above me, calling to tell me to '*Grab whatever you think you'll need to work from home for the next couple weeks and head for the gate*'.

A call like that might seem like an odd thing, but during my years at the lab, such things had become the norm.

I held both a Q and Top-Secret clearance and *that* put me in a class of lab employees that found themselves attached to all manner of project, most of which you couldn't talk about when you got home at the end of the day and your significant other asked '*How was your day?*'

Being sent home was tame. Finding yourself wandering around the recently drained Reflection Pool in Washington D.C. wearing a backpack full of radiation detection gear and an earpiece that crackled with the voice of an FBI team leader … That was the other end of the possibility spectrum in my line of work.

So, I grabbed an empty thumb drive and logged onto the intranet for the lab, then downloaded a pile of standard operating procedures that I was tasked with reviewing and updating as part of my busy work when nothing pressing was on my plate. These would do for whatever stint of 'work from home' was coming my way … or so I thought.

I logged off, locked down my CPU, locked down my office and made my way outside to the parking lot at the south-central sector of the 5300-acre complex that, while known to everyone who worked there as a government lab, those not from the area or well-versed in its history would know it simply as a very small town with no appreciable population, halfway out east on Long Island, in New York. There was a post office, a police station, a fire station, a water treatment plant, acres and acres of solar panels to supply our electricity needs and backup diesel generators just in case the sun decided to go down and stay down. Houses and apartments and a dormitory were there as well as a child development center, daycare, learning center, library, gym, indoor pool, cafeteria … Hell, we had a Starbucks and a bank.

But it wasn't a town.

It was a government installation. It began being so in 1918 when it became a training camp for the United States Military. Irving Berlin was stationed there when he wrote that song … You know the one.

There have been books written by people who worked there over the years, touting their possession of captured or downed UFOs and secret hangars filled with such things. There's even a place you can stand and do a Facebook Check In and it will say you're at the underground UFO storage facility. Rumors that The Majestic Twelve once were headquartered there persist to this day. But, again, for legal reasons, I won't name the place. Grab a map of Long Island and do a little detective work. You'll find it. Then type the name of the place into the Google search bar and watch the historic media explosion. Some of it is just plain silly media crap. Some of it, albeit exaggerated by the press, is absolutely true at the core. In summation, the place is and always has been steeped in mystery.

I was employed there by The Science Directorate for a very long time.

Again, I digress.

I left my office, thumb drive in my briefcase along with a few personal effects I didn't care to leave there overnight, let alone however long this stint would last.

I was waved down by a colleague in the parking lot after starting my vehicle and putting it in gear to leave. I rolled down the window as they came up near the driver's side.

"Any idea what's going on? They're closing the lab?"

"Corona Virus. It's been all over the news. I'm guessing we're being early adopters as usual. Better safe than sorry, right?"

Nick was animated as usual, but not in his usual jovial way. He shook with energy. The guy was in amazing shape for a man his age. He played an amazing rendition of *The Boxer* on acoustic guitar and was always in good spirits ... until now. This was the first time I'd seen him in any humor other than gleeful.

"Essential personnel ... *except* essential personnel ... *I'm* essential personnel. I'm not liking this ... Not one *bit* my friend."

"Fuck 'em. Go home."

"I'm up for funding review in two weeks. I can't."

I could see cars leaving other parking lots en masse and decided to take the time with Nick rather than join in what looked to be an accident waiting to happen.

"They told me to just grab enough work for a couple weeks. That could well be an indicator of how long they expect this will last before it peters out. For all we know, you won't even have white beam to work with once they put the accelerator in a safe condition and bring it down. I'm assuming that's the protocol still. You could just end up being sent home anyway once that's done."

He brightened a bit at that. But I'm not sure if his anxiety had lessened or if he just wanted me to feel that my efforts to be helpful had been successful. Either way, his demeanor went cheerful in an instant and he waved me off, stepping back from my vehicle.

"Spend some of your down time playing that amazing guitar! You'll have to bring it in again next time we're both on nights!"

He turned and began walking up Cornell at a brisk pace, hands thrust in his pockets and his head lower than I was used to seeing it. He didn't look back. He didn't wave. I took Temple down a block to the next intersection before heading for the gate, to avoid passing him as he walked, thus forcing another salutation.

I know what you're thinking.

'What happened to 'no names''?

That was the last time I saw Nick.

He died from Covid-19 six weeks after he was 'vaccinated'. Dead guys seldom sue.

I'm generally rather pragmatic about death. But this one stuck in my craw. You'll see why later on.

I made my way toward the security exit and, as I drove, I waved at those who waved and mimicked whatever emotion they displayed. Some smiled and waved. Some waved nervously. Everyone with whom I made eye contact waved in their fashion. And it was the last time I saw quite a few of them as well.

It was a Thursday. Traffic on the William Floyd Parkway was the usual fare. Sound Avenue heading east to where it turned into 48 was backed up for less than a mile. That was light for a weekday, but I had little experience with what the norm would be since I was always at the lab working at this time on a Thursday.

Breaking free of traffic for the 30 mile stretch through the vineyards and farm stands from the split to Calverton to Southold, I had entirely too much time to think. Cranking Pink Floyd's *The Final Cut* on the sound system helped a little, but the reactions I'd witnessed from my colleagues in their respective cars kept giving me cause to ponder. It was just a precaution. Hell, the lab closed if it snowed 3 inches out of an abundance of caution. I'd had no less than 50 paid days off due to nothing more than a little crappy weather. Everyone else had been through the same thing over the years and knew that knee-jerk closings were just par for the course. So why the worried looks ...?

Did some of them know things I didn't know?

By the ending explosion in *Fletcher Memorial Home* I'd managed to push it all to the back of my mind. I needed to be in a better state of mind when I presented myself to my live-in girlfriend Sam and our empathic, Greater Swiss Mountain Dog Baloo. No sense in bringing anything home from the lab that would have an adverse effect on anyone there.

I could hear the crunch of river rock under the tires as I pulled into the drive of our little cottage by the sea. Sam sat on the front steps, camera in hand, smiling a worried smile as I killed the engine and exited the vehicle.

"They closed the lab?"

"Yup."

"Covid?"

"Yup."

"Do I need to be worried?"

"Nope."

"I got some good shots of the hawk out over the salt marsh. I think he's hunting rabbits."

"Cool."

"Got some shots of a juvenile Golden Eagle on the beach earlier."

"Very cool."

"You sure we're okay?"

"Yah. You know how they are. Greatest minds in the world. Can't risk getting their butts sued off if anyone gets sick decides it's actionable. They shut it down if it snows. They just err on the side of conservatism no matter what."

"They're starting to shut other stuff down on the news."

"Fear mongers. Gotta do whatever they can to keep us glued to the boob tube. 'Don't touch that dial' and all that. We're fine. All the horse shit is happening back West. We're out East. Just another reason I took the place. There are a lot more advantages to living out here in the middle of nowhere than just having the ocean across the street."

She brightened. We were safe. She *believed* it for no other reason than that I'd said so.

And I was right. At that time, I had no idea just how much of a blessing it was to live out there. 75% of our neighbors only came out for the Summer. It was a pain in the ass during tourist season, but we did have a few private beaches to which I'd retained access after moving off Nassau Point, so solitude could be found even when the place was packed with foreigners and New York City, moneyed and entitled uber trash, who'd pay a hundred grand a month for anything that touched water and brag to their friends about it.

When things really got bad back West, the local authorities shut out the tourists and required proof of local residency to so much as park at any of the beaches or parks in the area.

But let's not get too far ahead of ourselves … We're not there yet …

Over the following two weeks, I did as I was instructed and worked from home. I updated and reviewed countless standard operating procedures and replied to any lab emails on my dot gov work Outlook account religiously. From all accounts, things were fine and we'd be back to the lab in no time. It remained so until the Sunday before the Monday I was to return to the lab.

The call from my departmental director went kind of like this:

"They're calling it Min-Safe Staffing. I guess the idea is to keep just the bare minimum number of people onsite so that critical operations and projects can continue without violating any fed regs. You, *blank* and *blank* will just rotate, two weeks on and four weeks off, with one of you at the lab Monday through Friday during normal hours while the other two stay home and get paid. Pretty sweet deal really."

"You know me. Whatever you need me to do, consider it done."

"Can you take the first rotation? You're the senior guy and frankly, it'd put my mind at ease if you were the first one in. You know, get everything lined up and in order before either of the other two have to come in and do their part."

"Not a problem. See ya tomorrow."

"No … I won't be there. They have me rotating with all the rest of the upper positions in our department. Only one of us will be on site at any given time. *Blank* will be there tomorrow, but he won't be out and about. He'll be in meetings off and on all day. If you need anything, you have my personal cell number and I'll be checking my office emails periodically … I really appreciate this …"

"No worries. You know the deal. You won't hear from me unless the lab catches fire. Enjoy your time away. I know I did."

And I had. The work from home thing for the past two weeks had afforded Sam and I plenty of time to take walks with Baloo on the beach and do a little touristing in Greenport just one town to the East of Southold. It was nice to forego the hour commute each way and spend the time saved doing things that didn't relate to the lab. Prior to that time, free time was in short supply and I was on call 24/7, so the distance we could go and how long we could stay had to be limited. Despite the grim reason for it all, the outcome had been a definite improvement.

Monday Came.

I was up at 05:45 as per Baloo's bladder and the alarm on my cell phone going off simultaneously. A quick trip out the back door off the sun porch that included a stroll through the back and side yards, leaf sniffing and the regular morning ablutions for him, then back inside for my routine of getting ready for work.

I dressed as I'd normally dress, taking into account the possibility of meetings popping up here and there to plan projects or design experimental processes, with shoes that were aimed more toward comfort while walking, with just enough of a professional appearance to be acceptable in a professional environment. Sometime in the middle of my preparations, Sam woke up and made her way to the kitchen for coffee. It was as regular as clockwork for a workday.

At exactly 7 am, I keyed the ignition of the Honda and put on my seatbelt before checking the rear view camera screen in the center of the dash, then throwing it into reverse. Although our house sat on a remote street just a block long between The North Road and the sea, people used it as a cut through more often than I liked, making for what I considered to be an unreasonable amount of traffic around this time of morning. But, on *this* morning, not a single vehicle was anywhere to be seen on the road for the first mile or so of my drive, let alone while I backed out to start my commute.

The drive amounted to roughly 37 miles total, varying by route. I occasionally hit the drive through at Burger King in Riverhead for a breakfast sandwich. That route brought me through a dozen or so traffic lights I wouldn't have to endure if I stuck to The North Road til Edwards Ave before turning south.

The nearly complete lack of traffic was at once a relief and a concern. It reminded me of driving to the convenient store on a holiday for milk and smokes when it was the only place open for miles. But it was Monday.

I decided to selze the opportunity to hit the Burger King, figuring the absence of traffic would ensure a very short wait time in line to get my food handed to me through the tiny window by the manager who resembled a high school football coach more than a fast-food restaurant boss. And I was right. As a matter of fact, I was the *only* person in the drive through line. There were no patrons inside at any of the booths I could see, and only three vehicles in the parking lot, presumably those of the employees. I ordered *two* loaded breakfast biscuits with the idea that I might be too busy to go offsite at lunch time to get anything later in the day. Again, I fully expected to be extremely busy all day, being the only representative for my entire department scheduled for the shift.

Roughly five minutes later I was back on the road and on track to arrive at the lab a few minutes early. Route 58, the main drag through Riverhead was all but deserted. Maybe thirty vehicles passed from any direction for the mile and a half distance to the end of town and the lanes being reduced down to just two for the remainder of the trip til the William Floyd Parkway. On a normal Monday there would have been hundreds. It was the main passage from The East End to the Long Island Expressway's first on ramp going west to The City.

Turning south on the William Floyd, I had only a few hundred yards until I'd reach the 'secret entrance', unmarked as access to the lab and only allowed for those of us who had the proper clearance to enter at that point. It was remote and nestled in the woods, with only one guardhouse and one security officer. If you swung too far to the right as you passed through, you'd literally hit a bunch of trees.

But, when I made the left across traffic, or rather the lack of traffic, the security gate was closed and the big cyclone fence entrance had been drawn to and locked up with chains and padlocks. I had to back out and drive back to the exit from which I'd come, make another left on Old Country Road and yet another left back onto the on ramp and down the three miles to the main gate. At the light I turned left. Sixty feet later, another light at which I went straight. The twin guardhouses loomed in the near distance just beyond the roundabout. Not a single vehicle was in line for access in front of mine.

When I pulled up and flashed my badge, the security officer, who knew me personally and had for over a decade, had me wait while he went back inside and checked his computer screen.

"They gave us a list of people who were allowed access. It's different every day now. You're on it Doc. Looks like it's your lucky day."

I thanked him and smiled. These were the guys who kept us all safe while we did our thing at the lab. All of them took their jobs very seriously and I appreciated that greatly. It made working at a known terrorist target a whole lot less stressful.

The drive from there to my office took several minutes. Each parking lot I passed, and there are many, was empty of anything that resembled a personal vehicle. Normally, on a Monday morning, even at this early hour, they would all be at least half full, filling up to capacity by 10 am when the last of us arrived.

The last time I had seen it like this was when I'd come in on Thanksgiving, living alone at the time and losing track of exactly which Thursday contained that holiday. Back then, security never gave me a second glance, even if I'd rolled up to the gate at three in the morning on Christmas. They knew the kind of odd hours scientists kept.

The lack of normalcy continued as I reached my building, parked in my spot and made for the entrance. The building was dark and locked down. Every morning prior to this one and that fateful Thanksgiving, I would be greeted by a well-lit, unlocked building and a member of the custodial staff offering a kind 'good morning Doc', asking if I'd had a good weekend or some other platitude. I think I took that for granted as a fixed sum to endure, with pleasantries in return regardless of my humor on any given day. Now, empty and dark, I missed those innocuous, morning meetings.

I used my site master key to open the building. I turned on the lights as I passed each switch on my way down to the last office on the left where I unlocked the door, stepped in and unshouldered my briefcase and hung it by the strap on the hall tree to the right. I turned on the lights and sat down in the big, comfortable office chair Uncle Sam had bought during the push for improved ergonomics among certain lab staff. I hadn't asked for it. It had simply shown up one day along with a thank you note.

It bordered on the embarrassing how the lab took care of me at times. Being born in deep poverty in 'the projects' and being raised for the most part in a simple, unmoneyed dynamic, being catered to was something I'd never grown used to in the least.

The next few hours were spent addressing departmental emails and sorting through interoffice mail that had piled up in my slot. I had a respiratory protection evaluation request that had been put in by the manager of custodial services for an evolution that involved spraying disinfectant agents in areas common areas to prevent the spread of 'the virus'.

The supervisor in charge of the evolution had asked if her staff could wear N95 dust masks instead of half or full face MSA respirators with P100 cartridges. Her reasoning was that the N95 masks didn't require a current fit test and that many on her staff did not have one, due to the person who performed said fit testing procedure working from home and being unavailable.

At the time, it seemed innocuous at best. The answer was simple. NIOSH, the agency that assigned Protection Factors to respiratory protection, had assigned a *zero* protection factor for the N95 and the manufacturer of said mask had been adamant about stating that it was only to be used for nuisance dust and silica. So, I denied the request and did the paperwork to assign the proper equipment for the job; and MSA Full Face Negative Pressure Facepiece with P100 HEPA filter cartridges.

You'd think that would have been the end of the discussion.

It was not.

Months later, when the subject reared its now ugly head again, Industrial Hygiene Management had written a procedure for fit testing employees on the N95 mask ... A mask that NIOSH had emphatically stated had a zero protection factor. A 50 was the minimum for anything to even be classified as effective against any substance that posed even a mild risk of adverse health effect.

This was coupled with the fact that the basic criteria for a fit test procedure to be conducted included being clean shaven on all sealing surfaces and an inspection to ensure there was no damage to the *seals* of the facepiece. There are no seals on a N95 mask. It's not even what one would consider a facepiece. And unless you used two sided tape to affix it to the wearer's face at every point of contact, there was no way to gat a seal. There was no way to do a negative pressure test which was also required by procedure prior to donning the mask.

It was ridiculous.

I said as much.

I was cut out of the loop for the remainder of the process as they went ahead and wrote the bogus procedure and proceeded to fit test every member of the custodial staff for a mask that provided zero protection factor, according to both the manufacturer and NIOSH.

Presently, if you check the NIOSH website, they have removed any and all mention of a lack of protection factor for the N95 mask and *recommend* it as a preventative measure for the spread of COVID-19.

Think about that.

Everyone on the planet has been told they are protected by wearing a dust mask that NIOSH tested and assigned no protection factor. After the CDC started telling people to wear them, NIOSH bowed out of the issue by simply removing that crucial information from their website. Procedures were authored that directly violated long-standing federal regulations, in order to employ a piece of personal protective equipment that was *known* to have no effect in the prevention of the spread of a virus.

Again, I digress, but this tangent is ever so germane to the progress of this telling. This was not the first lie the CDC put out as the gospel and it certainly wasn't the last.

Back to my first morning back at the lab after my two-week stint of working from home …

After all the administrative duties had been completed, I went back outside and hopped into my government issued Kubota and started making my usual rounds to the buildings in which I had project oversight. As I drove around, each parking lot I passed was empty still and not a single soul was seen out and about. On a normal Monday, by nearly noon, in weather such as this, the place would look like a college campus quad with people walking in groups and eating out of doors and holding photo sessions for the press in front of signs that touted this project or that.

I found each and every building I attempted to access locked up tight with the lights out. The cafeteria was closed. The gym and indoor pool were closed as well. The only places I could find that showed signs of life were the post office, firehouse and security posts. With those few exceptions, the 5300-acre complex had taken on the appearance of a post-apocalyptic movie set.

If anyone other than those few people *were* there, they had shut themselves away in their respective offices and locked the doors behind them.

For all intents of purpose, I was alone.

It continued in this manner for the span of two weeks. I arrived on time. I busied myself with what I could find to do. I spoke to no one. I saw no one other than security. My phone did not ring. My email was all but lifeless with only the occasional check in from a colleague or two, asking if I was doing okay. I was beginning to feel like the unwitting subject of one of our own experiments.

On the second Friday afternoon, my cell phone rang. On the other end was my departmental director. He informed me that my relief for the coming Monday had declared themselves 'at risk' and would be unable to report for duty.

He asked if I could 'tough it out' for another two-week stint.

I answered to the effect of 'I'm getting paid either way. I might as well be here'.

He was both apologetic and grateful. The deal was struck and the schedule amended.

When I arrived home, Sam was none too happy. She said it wasn't fair. I answered in kind with the stipulation that I *was* being paid and that showing up was the least I could do. I also added that part of my extreme success in securing and keeping employment over the span of my long career had a lot to do with my work ethic. We lived a very good life that was financed by a monthly paycheck, provided by the lab, that never bounced and had lots of zeroes on it. Doing them this favor could do nothing short of ensuring the continuation of that dynamic.

We enjoyed the weekend as much as we could with the limitations of the now pandemic as obstacles. No indoor dining. Lines outside every kind of store due to occupancy limitations. Limited availability of retail items due to hoarding and supply chain logistics issues.
But traffic was light, and we could drive about the East End and enjoy looking at the mansions and beaches. We walked the private beach at Nassau Point with Baloo and ordered amazing Guatemalan food from the joint down the street over the phone and picked it up at curbside from a little man who didn't look in the least worried about any of the other things going on. He was just really happy to have the business.

Then Monday. Another uneventful week at the lab, followed by another almost identical weekend and another Monday.

And, at roughly 1 pm, the phone in my office rang.

Building 463. Biology Building. Laboratory number *blank.*

The person on the other end spoke broken English but my years at the lab had greatly improved my ability to converse in that dialect.

He'd been assigned to work on 'a vaccine' and required my oversight in planning and designing the processes necessary to conduct the initial phases of the research.

Finally. Something to do other than twiddle my thumbs and roam the grounds.

We set up an initial meeting for the next day at 10 am. It was odd that the request hadn't come down from my departmental director. The normal protocol was to put in a request for help and that would filter through upper management, and *they* would decide who to assign to the project after determining which scientist had the best fit as far as qualifications, security clearances and skillset most conducive to the success of the project. In my mind, there was no need for all that since I was not only the most qualified in my department … I was the *only* one present and available. There was no reason to question any of it from where I stood.

It never occurred to me to ask what the vaccine we were planning to create was *for*.

It certainly couldn't be for COVID-19. It was a virus. And anyone with a reasonable background in medical science knows that you can't create a vaccine for a virus of that kind. Viruses of that kind simply mutate into something else when they are attacked. Something that can survive whatever is attacking it. And it was a well-known fact that medical science had been trying since roughly 1972 to come up with an effective vaccine for the Corona Virus (the root cause of the common cold) and had met with zero success. It had been a waste of resources in the end. And, of course, COVID-19 was just the most recent iteration of The Corona Virus.

With that in mind, I finished my shift and went home.

Tuesday morning came … 10 am came … and brought with it a very bad surprise …

"You do realize there is no way to make a vaccine for COVID-19 … It's a mutating virus. You know the logistics. You know the previous attempts. You know it can't be done."

"I know all these thing. I'm told come up with solution. This what we do, yes?"

I just stood and stared at him. I guess I was waiting for him to smile and say he was just pulling my leg or to impart some previously unknown scientific fact that would make him sound less like an idiot. I don't mean to be an ass about it, but these guys were supposed to be 'some of the greatest minds in the world' and I was getting a little tired of having that phrase come back to haunt me. It was part of the pitch that had been used to get me to sign on permanently at the lab well over a decade ago when I switched from contractor to 'in house'.

After a few moments and no change in his position, I decided to take a different tack.
"We could come up with a *treatment* to reduce the expression of symptoms in the infected … At best we could isolate the chemical signal that prompts the protein expression for the RNA replication and mute it …"

"They want vaccine."

"*They* can want til the cows come home. That won't make the impossible become possible. Do you *not* understand that?"

"They tell me make vaccine. You help, yes?"

Far too much time was being wasted, but, in my mind, I had nothing *but* time while I was at the lab these days. The very least I could do was *try* to at least steer this project in a productive direction.

We agreed to step back from the meeting and regroup in a week, at which time we would hopefully have culled more information with which to work.

That Friday evening, while I was at home, an email came in from a project director and primary investigator from one of the accelerators, asking if I had come up with anything on the Building 463 Project. Being that he was also involved in several projects I'd overseen in the Biology Department, I replied with the best Idea I'd come up with so far since Tuesday.

'Treat it in the same manner we treat a malignant tumor. We need to come up with the equivalent of anti-angiogenesis treatments to mute the chemical signal it sends out to initiate RNA replication. Break up the blueprint it sends so that it can't be read by the receiver.'

He wrote back asking for a more in-depth explanation and I responded with as much as I had worked out in my head up to that point.

I waited for his response.

None came.

I heard nothing ... Not from him ... Not from the guy in building 463 with whom I'd met the previous Tuesday ... Not a peep.

My rotation ended without further incident. Having heard nothing from Biology and not having permission to turn over any projects due to oversight continuity protocols, I left for my two weeks off and did my best not to give it much more thought.

Over my two weeks off from the lab, getting paid to do absolutely nothing, Sam and I spent the majority of our time watching the world back west fall apart. Access to 24-hour news stations was something relatively new, but the networks had most definitely caught on quickly. Around the clock coverage of death tolls and statistics and the ever-present face of Anthony Fauci flapping his gums about what people should and shouldn't be doing. And our tv was on the entire time we were awake every single day.

At first, Fauci was telling people to stop wearing masks because they didn't work, and they gave people a false sense of protection and increased the speed at which the virus was spreading. *Then* he did a 180 and started telling everyone to wear one … then eventually two … then stay six feet apart … And any time anyone questioned his waffling on any number of 'facts', he would accuse them of attacking science or being science deniers because 'to question me is to question science' … Sounds a lot like something a 12th century priest would say to the masses if they questioned a bit of supposed doctrine.

There were entire states at odds with mask mandates or lack thereof. Federal funding was being given or withheld depending on the level of compliance with the ever changing 'rules' being passed down from different government entities. The stock market was taking a nosedive.

While I always prefer time away from work and with Sam, getting back to the lab and away from the television news was starting to be something to which I looked forward.

I'm sure the things being shown and said were a welcome source of much needed information for the vast majority of the world, but when you *know* how much of it is patently untrue, it is just a source of constant irritation.

And Fauci?

What a horrid little Chihuahua of a man. No matter what he said on the tv, right, wrong or in direct conflict with facts, or even if it was the exact opposite of something he'd said just days before, he *demanded* that everyone take his word as the gospel. He was regularly lying to our faces and daring anyone to call him on it. And if anyone *did* call him on it or disagree in any way, they were immediately labeled as an idiot. Literally *thousands* of trained medical professionals were regularly refuting his claims and backing it up with real data, but it either fell on deaf ears, was intentionally not covered by the media or dismissed as the ravings of a right-wing science denier. It was sickening.

In June, the family from whom we leased our little cottage by the sea, came out from Queens for the Summer. They were a married couple with four sons. Both husband and wife were NYC school teachers. Queens was one of the 'hot spots' on the high infection rate map, put out by the CDC. With all that was going on back west, Sam and I decided to forego our usual social interactions with the lot of them for the first few weeks they were there in order to ensure that if any of them had been infected, it wouldn't end up being passed along to us.

Going back … The previous November had been a bad month. There was no mention of the Corona Virus being an issue in the US at that time, so when we both came down with what can only be described as a bad case of the flu, I just burned some sick time and stayed home from work while we toughed it out and waited for the symptoms to subside. And they did. But, looking back, it is highly likely that both of us were infected with COVID-19 at that time and just didn't have any reason to think that's what we had.

In January, 2020 came the first 'reported' case of the virus. Statistically, that means it was likely in our country for many months prior to that time. With 75% of infected people being either without symptoms or simply having what mimicked the common flu, and the virus not being tested for at that early stage (we didn't *have* a test for it in November) there is no way of knowing how many cases occurred through 2019.

Anyway, this lends itself to the probability that Sam and I were both already teeming with antibodies against COVID-19 and at little or no risk of contracting it again any time soon. I was exposed to thousands of people during the pre-lockdown period. People from all over the world. And I brought that home each evening from the lab. We regularly went out to eat, shopped local stores and had conversations with random people from our neighborhood while out for walks in those days.

So, when we finally did feel it was safe to interact with our friends from Queens, the odds are that we were already adequately protected against infection.

As a matter of fact, the odds are that roughly 75% of the population on the east coast were probably in the same boat. Flu season from 2019 had probably been filled with all kinds of people with COVID-19 who were diagnosed with other ailments because, again, there was no test for COVID-19 at that time and it was not in the diagnostic pool to be chosen until much later.

By July, things at the lab had lightened up a bit and the number of people coming to work increased quite a bit. But there were protocols to be observed. 100% masking all the time unless you were alone in your office with the door closed. Even if you were out walking down the sidewalk you were expected to mask up. Face to face meetings were avoided whenever possible. A lot of routine work that had previously been performed on a regular periodicity, was set aside and done only on an as needed basis.

It was during those times that I engaged in some rather interesting conversations with colleagues who, as it turns out, were like-minded about the whole situation. The federal government was throwing money at vaccine research in a manner never before seen. But the majority of us already knew the logistics against making a vaccine for *any* virus, let alone this one. The idea that the N95 mask suddenly had the ability to stop a virus when, just a few short months earlier it wasn't trusted to protect workers against inhaling bird shit was a suspicious event across the board and the subject of many a conversation among the scientific community.

I kept my work in building 463 to myself as it was becoming more and more clear that some of the things that went on during the absence of practically everyone else, had not been meant for common knowledge. It did however remain as a nagging little voice at the back of my head that had nothing good to say about the whole thing.

The Summer was just strange. Away from the lab, life had taken on an air of the unfamiliar. No crowds of tourists. The local governments had made mandates that people to the west of us needed to stay where they were instead of performing their ritual migration out east, carrying with them the greatly increased likelihood of spreading the infection that was so prevalent in their areas. There were actual lawsuits lodged against the towns by the owners of summer homes out our way who were being denied access to them. People who had taken on Winter rentals were refusing to vacate the homes they had rented, even though their lease had been limited to occupancy only through June.

*It is a common practice in The Hamptons and areas of that type, to rent out one's home for the Winter/off season months at a greatly reduced rate, in order to keep it occupied, heated and watched over, at no expense to the owners. A home that goes for $1200 a month in Winter can go for as much as $50,000 a month in Summer.

Locals were also railing against those who *had* come out to their Summer homes before the restrictions had been put in place because they tended to go to the local grocery stores and buy everything in sight to stock up for the Summer. And they were doing the same thing this go round with the pandemic in mind and the possibility that they would be staying far longer than their usual stint on the east end. With the lack of adequate stocking of shelves in most stores, this practice was seen as hoarding.

I, on the other hand, had discovered a rather large, well-stocked grocery store at the eastern edge of Riverhead in a less than desirable neighborhood. It seemed that no one who 'had money' would be caught dead in such a place out of fear for their safety or their reputation, so the prices remained low and the parking lot mostly empty. I went there regularly to get all of the things we couldn't find anywhere else. Fresh fruit, toilet paper and all the rest of the grocery items that had fallen into short supply everywhere else, could be found in abundance at this store.

As the world fell apart everywhere around us, we once again found ourselves insulated against most of it due to our financial situation and geographical location in a low population density area.

The East End became the place to be. But we were not the only people who had come to that realization.

The value of real estate in and around 'The City' took a nosedive and anything that was in an area of less dense population saw a sharp increase in housing prices. If it was within striking distance of NYC but rural, rents doubled and home values went up double or more in many cases. And it was spreading across the country within a short time. There was a mass exodus from large cities by those in a position to afford such a move and those on the selling end were taking full advantage of their position by charging every penny the market would bear.

The large, rural land holdings many families had accumulated and held over generations soon sold out at extreme prices to developers who meant to take advantage of the situation as well. There was a construction boom the likes of which our country hadn't seen since the end of WW2.

But, at that time, our little slice of the East End remained unaffected by the majority of it.

At work, things were becoming more and more strange by the day. Due to occupancy limitations in the building where my regular office was located, I was asked to move my things to my secondary office in the chemistry building, a rather remote location with no windows and zero cell phone reception. But it put me in closer proximity to the work I was doing, so it wasn't so much a hardship as a blessing in many ways. It did, however remove me from the decision-making hub of our department. At the time I considered it a welcome relief from being involved on a near constant basis with such things. In the end, it became apparent that I had been removed from that dynamic for a reason.

My stance on a *lot* of the COVID-related issues and associated procedures, was in direct conflict with 'the company line' as it were. Requested revisions to the way we did business were in direct conflict with long-standing federal regulations and I'd put my proverbial foot down on quite a few occasions when asked to weigh in on said decisions. When they moved me to chemistry, they stopped involving me in any of it.

My two company vehicles were taken away due to a new lab policy against multiple occupants in said vehicles. It was considered an exponential increase in the likelihood of infection being passed from one person to the next if we used the same vehicle as others without having it disinfected first. This was considered an unreasonable expense, so the use of lab provided transportation was all but done away with for all but upper management. The rest of us were expected to use our personal vehicles to navigate the 5300-acre complex and perform out duties.

Again, I didn't really care. I actually came to prefer it. The only time you were mandated to use a government vehicle was if you were transport instrumentation that contained a radioactive check source. And, when the weather was nice, I preferred to walk on such occasions anyway.

I announced to my supervision in August that I would be retiring the coming May.

The whole thing was just getting to be a bit much and my investments had proven to be well-placed and the return on them had positioned us to be comfortable without my monthly paycheck from the lab. The advanced notice was given in an effort to give them time to assign someone to me to be mentored and brought up to speed on what I did and how to do it in my eventual absence.

Giving said advanced notice turned out to be a bad decision.

At first, they took the kind approach. I was given The Spotlight Award for my contribution to science. It came with a big fat bonus check. And I was given the biggest raise I'd gotten in my entire career. I was asked to please consider staying on for a bit longer than my May, 2021 projection. I was called in to the departmental director's office and thanked for my service and was asked if there was anything the lab management could do to make me more happy with my employment with the science directorate.

It was as if all of the dissent over my disagreements with recent decisions had been forgotten and I was once again considered 'the golden boy' of the department.

After an evening at home with Sam to discuss the extension to our timeline, the decision was made to just continue going in to work until such time as I no longer felt like doing so. I said nothing to anyone at work about it. It was to my advantage to allow them to labor under the assumption that I would always be just one bad day away from leaving.

On December 12th, the big story in the news was 'the vaccine' … It was being shipped out to all the states in quantities large enough to start vaccinating the public en masse.

And on the next day I was at the lab, I found myself roaming the halls, looking in each laboratory until I found the one to which my project partner for the development of the impossible vaccine had been moved.

We had lunch.

We discussed the impossible logistics of not only the impossible vaccine but the impossibly short time it had taken to garner approval from the FDA, a process that should have taken years, not just a few months.

According to him, in the best English he could muster, he had been removed from the project about a month after I had. His insistence that their endeavor was in vain and that the funding could be put to better use working on a treatment for the infected rather than being wasted on an impossible pursuit ... basically the conclusion we had drawn during our meeting many months ago ...

As he continued filling me in, he became more and more agitated about the whole thing. He brought up the point that the latency period for potential side effects could be years and that the clinical trials couldn't have possibly been completed in keeping with FDA requirements.

Let me clarify that for those who may not have a medical background and never worked in a research environment ... Let's take a look at how we screwed up as a scientific community when it came to the adverse health effects of exposure to ionizing radiation.

Marie Curie lost a finger ... then later died from the latent effects of her repeated exposure to Radium, the element she basically discovered and studied long term.

This is classified as the result of a long term, chronic exposure. The exposures she subjected herself to on a daily basis we large, but none of them alone were enough to cause an immediate, observable adverse health effect. Over time though, the effects of these exposures added up and their collective detrimental effect resulted in her death in the long term.

An acute exposure to ionizing radiation, like the ones suffered by workers trying to put out the graphite fires at the Chernobyl Nuclear Plant in Russia, resulted in their respective deaths, all within 30 days and all as the result of one very large exposure.

A latent effect (latency period) is an adverse health effect that can take decades to express symptoms. People who were working in Uranium processing facilities during the 1940's through the 1990's have been being diagnosed with cancer at an alarming rate, 35 years after their exposures to ionizing radiation. There just wasn't enough data associated with exposures to radiation for science to have any idea about the long term effects of certain kinds of exposures until enough time had passed after said exposures to observe the resulting adverse health effect. In this case, cancer.

And, for the longest time, the federal government resisted taking responsibility for the dramatic increase in the cancer rate among those workers, stating that there were too many other environmental factors that could have been the cause of those cancers. Later, in recent decades, after being presented piles and piles of data that proved radiation was the most likely cause, The Atomic Energy Workers Act came into existence and set aside billions of dollars to address the issue and compensate workers and/or their survivors for what they had done to them decades prior.

It has been since determined that the latency period for cancer due to exposure to ionizing radiation can be as long as 35 years.

35 years ... They didn't have *one* year's worth of data on the potential side effects of any vaccine, let alone what the long term, latent effects might be. If there is some horrible latent adverse health effect of the 'vaccines' being pumped into the arms of anyone they can get their hands on, that doesn't express symptoms for a year ... 5 years ... 10 years ... or 35, they *can't* know what they are because they didn't go through the necessary FDA protocols for testing.

It took over 10 years of studies and data before the FDA approved *Tylenol*.

Think about that for a minute.

And Tylenol is an over-the-counter drug that people only take when they have symptoms that need treatment germane to the abilities of that drug.

The current 'vaccines' are being given to *everyone*. Not just those who need it … everyone.

The idea *we* had for a treatment for those infected with the COVID-19 virus, ensured that the only people who would receive said treatment would be those who *needed* it due to *being infected*. This would have meant that those who were bad enough off to be brought to the hospital for *treatment* would be pretty much guaranteed not to have a fatal outcome, so long as treatment was administered at an early enough stage.

This would eliminate treating those who were already immune, those who only expressed mild symptoms and those who had not been infected at all.

We discussed how they were going to figure out who to give this so-called vaccine, when only 25% of the population would even contract the virus and express severe symptoms. Considering the dangers of exposing *everyone* to a vaccine with so little data history, we thought for certain it would be a limited roll-out, aimed at those with pre-existing co-morbidity factors … The elderly, those who were immunocompromised due to existing illness or cancer treatment … Those would be the people for whom the roll of the proverbial dice would be worth the risk.

"They can't give it to kids."

I agreed.

The likelihood of adverse health effect due to exposure to ionizing radiation is exponentially increased as the cellular division rate increases. Children have the highest cellular division rate of our species. The younger they are, the higher their cellular division rate. The higher the cellular division rate, the more likely it is that some of those divisions will be subject to mutation.

In the end, we took the optimistic viewpoint and hoped this 'vaccine' would be used as a preemptive therapeutic measure to kick start people's immune systems in anticipation of an infection.

We left it at that.

We were sadly mistaken.

After the November elections, things got worse. While the stock market had gained back everything it had lost due to the virus and the associated closures of so many businesses and supply chains being stressed, when Biden took office, it lost nearly half its value again.

And our new President had a plan ... 100 million vaccines administered by June.

Why?

What in the hell was the big hurry getting a virtually untested syringe full of crap into that many arms that quickly? If anything, you'd think they would be proceeding with an abundance of caution.

Instead, the federal government was throwing every dollar they could get at a solution that was *not* a solution. Frankly, it scared the shit out of more than half the scientific community who understood the potential dangers of doing so.

Imagine coming up with a radical, experimental cure for cancer that had a slim chance of being beneficial to a dying patient … a long shot … a roll of the dice … And then having the federal government decide that it was going to be given to *everyone*, just in case some of them might have cancer somewhere in their body that hadn't been found.

Because *that* is what this so-called vaccine is.

And here's the worst part …

The known course of any large-scale epidemic plays out like this …

First wave has an extremely high mortality rate due to those who were already dying of something unrelated or had co-morbidity issues sufficient to make the new illness enough to kill them. During this first wave, many will be infected and survive and acquire the resulting antibodies and associated immunity to the illness. Yet more will be infected and never know they had it. Those people already had a natural immunity which is now boosted due to being exercised by contracting the illness, albeit without expressing observable symptoms.

Second wave will cause a fatal outcome for those who have developed co-morbidity issues in the interim since the first wave sufficient to have that effect. Those who have become ill from unassociated causes will be at higher risk of a fatal outcome. But the death toll for the second wave will be exponentially less than the first wave.

Third wave … There may not be a third wave that is readily observable statistically due to the improved immunity of those infected during the first two waves who survived, *unless* the epidemic is associated with a *virus* that is caused to mutate by some outside influence.

We are currently in the third wave. And we have been attacking this virus with an outside agent, apart from the natural immunity *all survivors would have developed without a vaccine* … and it has done exactly what this type of viruses do … mutate.

As of November 17th, 2022, according to Yale Medicine, *eight* prominent variants of COVID-19 have been identified. That means there are most likely twice that many.

Guess how many there would be if we hadn't 'vaccinated' everyone.

One.

The root of COVID-19 is The Corona Virus … The common cold. The common cold virus has remained relatively unchanged for … well for as long as we've been able to scientifically observe it and accumulate data … outside the laboratory environment. And, as a result, the human species has developed enough natural immunity to the common cold that it is incredibly rare for that virus to cause a fatal outcome unless it is contracted by someone with co-morbidity issues sufficient to cause said outcome.

Sound familiar?

As for the common cold … the Corona Virus *inside a lab environment* over the past 6 decades or more? We've been screwing with it, attacking it, forcing it to mutate, attempting to weaponize it, trying to create an impossible vaccine for it, trying to figure out how to make money off it … But that is in a lab environment … A strictly controlled, impeccably contained set of experiments with safety protocols out the wazoo and associated federal regulations that would make your head spin …

It's safe.

Until it's not safe anymore.

People fuck up.

People become complacent about safety protocols.

People make *reasonable assumptions* about the *real* risks involved with their research.

And in countries other than the US, regulations can be either far more strict or not exist at all.

And they're all doing the same kinds of research.

Part of this is from our conversation over lunch. Part of it is information that has come to light since then.

Again, I digress. But it was germane to the subject matter.

When Fall came, our neighbors made the move back to Queens as the school year was starting and all six of them would be in attendance; four students and two teachers. They would however find that the age of online classes would be the lion's share of their respective school years.

The children who did attend classes in person were made to wear masks at all times unless they were *eating* … An example of the complete and utter lack of logic being applied to the mask mandates. Parents railed against the schools for the discomfort the children were being put through in order to attend school. Many kept their children at home. Many switched over to home schooling. Psychologists went on and on about how that dynamic would retard the development of the children's social skills.

People in general had an extreme reduction in social interaction and when they did meet 'face to face' all they saw was the mask. All they heard were muffled words. And all anyone wanted to talk about was the virus. It caused wide-spread disassociation between human beings and the instances of mental illness climbed in never before seen fashion.

People were dying in droves, but it seemed that the reports from hospitals of people dying from pretty much *anything else* had been reduced to nothing. Records were being skewed intentionally to garner a larger share of the federal tax dollars that were being doled out in keeping with the reported numbers for COVID-19 related deaths and hospitalizations. If you died of pneumonia and tested positive for COVID-19 after the fact, they would attribute your death to COVID-19. It was reported that in some cases, even fatalities from vehicle accidents who were either dead on arrival or died while in the care of the hospital at a later date, they would chalk it up to COVID-19 to bolster their numbers.

One evening, while watching the never-ending news with Sam, the death toll became the subject of a rather lengthy and contentious conversation.

She believed that if the vaccine would save lives, it should be given to everyone.

I agreed, with the stipulation that, that would only hold true if it actually was a vaccine. A vaccine, once administered, is supposed to *prevent* infection altogether. What was coming out from the three major players in big pharma, was not in fact, a vaccine.

I explained that since viruses mutated when attacked, a true vaccine for a virus of this kind was impossible. She knew that viruses mutated, but had not gone down that rabbit hole of what happens when they do.

I went on to expound on something that came from a very pragmatic place ...

Every now and then, 'nature' sends something our way that challenges the survival of a species. It's how immune systems are enhanced and how adaptations to environmental variables strengthen a species. It's part of the process of evolution. This applies to *all* species, humans included. And throughout our evolution from basic primate, through the Ice Age and up to modern day, there have been many instances where, had we not been challenged and forced to adapt, we would not have made it to where we are now as a species. And I added that, if COVID-19 didn't turn out to be an extinction event, it too would strengthen our species by culling the weak and infirm, leaving only those strong enough to survive and adapt, to breed.

She wasn't fond of that viewpoint. I was accused of being callous and my autism was brought in as the only reason I was able to see it that way.

I defended my position as best as I could without the evidence that supports it that has since been uncovered.

And … had we left the damn virus alone and allowed the culling to happen in the manner it was supposed to happen, it would be over with by now. Instead, we have an even higher death toll and eight friggen strains attacking the world, seven of which we caused to exist by attacking the first one and all of the subsequent variants.

My argument back then, as it is now, is that everyone needs to just become infected and, in doing so, either develop natural immunity to it or die from it. The death rate would be the same and the outcome would be the same, minus trillions of dollars wasted fighting something we can't prevail against and creating more of the same in multiple variants that will then have to be suffered through as well.

My colleague from building 463 and I had opted for the Chinese joint in Ridge. There was no place to eat on site and this place had actually opened their dining room to limited occupancy in booths that were separated by 15 feet or so. It made for a nice escape from the lab and the distance between booths added to the privacy we sought.

At the conclusion of our nearly 3-hour lunch break, we drove back to the lab in our respective vehicles.

Since my office was now a good quarter of a mile from anyone who might want to keep tabs on my comings and goings, my extended lunch went unnoticed. It was now after 3 pm and I spent the remaining hour and a half of my shift rummaging through anything COVID related I could find on the CDC website, government clearance partition, that could only be accessed via the intranet connection provided to those of us with a need to access it. This is the part with the databases not available to the general public.

I didn't find anything that was helpful. I didn't find anything that might disprove our suspicions. It was not a well-populated database at that time and I found that a little unsettling.

With all the claims I was hearing Fauci making on tv, I figured there had to be some data to back it up.

None.

Nothing.

This chuckle-head was shooting from the hip and defying anyone to ask for proof … because he had none. There were no studies that showed any reason why people should feel protected by *any* kind of mask, let alone the flimsy 'face coverings' that had become more popular than the N95 and more widely accepted. There was no mention of how long it took in close proximity to an infected individual to become infected. There was no data that substantiated his claim that people should wear nitrile gloves while out and about. There was no data backing up his fear-mongering claims about the virus laying about for days on dry surfaces, waiting to infect the first person who touched said surface.

It was almost like this guy owned stock in the mask and glove companies, ya know?

Common knowledge among people with a background in medical science: No moisture, no virus. Period. It's impossible for a virus to survive in a moisture-free environment. If it lands on a dry countertop, the moment the moisture in which it was travelling evaporates, it dies.

By the way … in real time, as I write this line on November 30th, 2022, it is known that it requires roughly 15 minutes in close proximity to an infected person, engaged in constant conversation, while facing one another, to effectively transmit the COVID virus. If they sneeze in your face however, the transmission can be immediate.

The approximated incubation period for you to begin expressing symptoms and for you to be contagious, can range from one to two weeks, depending on your general health and individual physiology. That's why it was so maddening to hear on the news about how a child's family birthday party with 35 children in attendance three days ago, was the cause of an outbreak … a 'super spreader event' …

Fear mongering.

It became the go-to leverage device when trying to reinforce the idea that people needed to comply or they would be in immediate danger of contracting this horrible, extremely contagious killer virus ... What a load of horse crap.

I still can't find any *real* science that substantiates over half of what we were told to fear.

Then came Winter ... and with it, the vaccine mandates.

It was frightening.

People were losing their much-needed jobs because they dared to refuse to be vaccinated. Even though there was no real scientific data that supported its approval for use ... no in-depth clinical trials of anything one might consider a reasonable time period ... and no culpability for the government or any of the big pharma companies who were pumping the vaccines out ...

Let me put that another way ... *People who could not be held accountable if the vaccine killed every single person who got it, were mandating that everyone get it and threatening to take away your source of income if you didn't.*

But ... if you were poor and ignorant and afraid that the government didn't have your best interest in mind, the 'stimulus checks' were being doled out to reassure you who had your back.

However, if your income was such that it was likely you were a critical thinker and/or had a college level education and a reasonable IQ, no check for you. It would be a waste of their money and they knew it. You were one of the demographic they knew they couldn't buy, so they resorted to threats of taking away everything you'd spent your life working for, forcing your businesses to close and limiting your ability to even travel about the country to make your living.

It was becoming more clear with each passing day that the governments of the world were seizing this opportunity to flex on the general population. It was a new form of leverage. It was an amazing cash cow. It was a way to come out looking like saviors and heroes who protected them against the killer virus … Even thought not one single thing they did saved a single life. The death toll is currently even higher than it would have been if everyone had just sat back and kept their hands in their pockets for the first year. The people who were going to die, died anyway. The new strains that were born out of the attacks on the original strain were later able to take even more lives due to being able to overcome the natural immunity the infected from the first wave had developed. The current death toll total is 6,638,940 worldwide. That number could have probably been cut in half if the 7 subsequent variants hadn't been created with our meddling.

If you think for one minute that the so-called vaccines have kept anyone from becoming infected, you're wrong. It prevented nothing. But it took credit for everything. Your immunity? Your ability to go about your day without becoming infected? All naturally occurring due to your long-term, chronic exposure to low levels of the virus in the air you breathe and the things you eat and drink. None of it had anything to do with being vaccinated.

Proof?

The unvaccinated aren't dying.

At this point in time, vaccinated and unvaccinated people have the same level of immunity to the virus.

Tens of thousands of people however *have* died due to an adverse reaction to the *vaccine*, without ever having contracted the 'killer virus'.

From December, 2020 through today, December 1st, 2022, around 5.4 billion people have been vaccinated world wide and if booster shots are added into the equation, over 12 *billion* doses of vaccine have been administered across a world population that just hit 8 billion a short time ago.

If ever someone wanted to see an example of world governments controlling the actions of the world population, there you have it.

This wasn't a case of '*Hey guys! We have this vaccine that we have made available for free and, if you want it, we'll give it to you.*' This was, in far too many cases, the result of bullying, shaming, threats of being fired from your job, drummed out of the military with a dishonorable discharge, removal of your right to travel to visit loved ones or conduct business … If you didn't *want* the vaccine, you were in for one hell of a fight.

And *testing* for the virus and its many variants? The latest number I can squeeze out of the internet is around 72 billion tests sold/handed out to the public at a cost of roughly $15/test minimum.

Somebody is paying for those tests, even if you have been getting them for free.

And someone … is getting paid.

And that's just home test kits. I couldn't get a hard number of tests that have been administered by medical professionals to the public worldwide. If we are to be extremely conservative, you can double the number of home tests just to get an idea … 144 *billion* COVID tests … at a conservative estimated cost of $15/test … Across the board, just on COVID *testing* over $2.16 *TRILLION* dollars has changed hands.

A rough estimate of the money involved in treatment, vaccine administration, manufacturing and transportation, federal funding handed out, relief funds issued, grants approved and other incidental expenses associated with COVID other than testing … $11 trillion dollars has changed hands over a two year period.

Over $13 trillion dollars … has changed hands in the past 2 years in association with COVID … You'd think money moving on that scale would stimulate the economy. It's more money than the net worth of the entire 1% we've been taught to fear and hate … If you take the top ten thousand wealthiest people on the planet and lump together their net worth, you don't get $13 trillion dollars.

So … how are we in a worldwide recession right now?

If that kind of money has been circulating through the world economy on top of all the non-COVID-related money that was already changing hands … why do we have the highest inflation rates in history and people scraping to get by from the burger flipper to the welder to the farmer to the store clerk?

The.

Money.

Went.

Somewhere.

You'd think, 'Wow … Now they have all kinds of money to train new healthcare professionals and buy the best equipment available to update and improve their ability to provide the best medical care possible …'

Considering how many medical professionals refused to be vaccinated and subsequently lost their jobs because of it, the part about needing to train a lot of new healthcare professionals rings true. The rest of it, not so much.

You'd think that the unemployment rate would drop to nothing with all the new jobs being created in association with the testing and treatment of COVID and the manufacture and sales of things that went along with it …

Nope.

I've looked high and low for some positive effect brought on by the movement of such a huge sum of money through the economy.

I can't find one.

Wars are, believe it or not, huge economic stimulators. After WW2 came a couple of decades that brought on a period of financial growth and prosperity that propelled an entire generation into the middle class. And it is estimated that, in today's dollars, that war caused about $4.1 trillion dollars to change hands.

So, you figure, triple that number for the current economy and population and … nothing. Nothing positive anyway.

The world in general has seen an overall financial downturn since the beginning of the whole Pandemic, regardless of the money that has been changing hands throughout the whole mess.

We're on the last leg of it.

It should be all over with by late Spring 2023, or so they're predicting.

So why aren't there an amazing number of people being propelled into the middle class? Why aren't there an amazing number of new home starts and new businesses popping up left and right and thriving due to the dramatic increase in discretionary income possessed by all because of the great stimulation of the world economy …?

I don't have the answer.

I have ideas, but they sound an awful lot like things a conspiracy theorist might think. They sound an awful lot like we, as a world population, have just spent a couple of years being the victims of the largest, most evil cash grab in the history of mankind.

Late Spring, 2022 … Get the vaccine or your employment at the government lab will be terminated … unless you filed a religious exemption … then we'll give you an extra 30 days to give up your religious beliefs and get the vaccine … unless you have a valid medical exemption that says you will most likely experience and adverse health effect if vaccinated … then you have 60 days to get your shit together and get over whatever it is, and get your vaccine … or your fired … Once you have provided proof of your complete vaccination, you will be issued a special badge on a special shade of blue lanyard to wear around your neck at all times while you are on lab property … the vaccine is *not* available onsite and will *not* be provided by the lab for reasons of legal liability …

This was the gist of what we were all being told at the lab. 'Some of the greatest minds in the world' were being told by management that they had to go offsite and get a shot or series of shots for a vaccine that we all knew couldn't exist … and that neither the lab nor the federal government nor the manufacturers of the vaccines could be held responsible for adverse outcome from the vaccine … but you had to get it or your employment would be terminated.

The attrition rate at the lab exploded.

I wrote an email to my departmental director stating that I was opposed to getting the vaccine and exactly why. I based it on nothing more than not liking having a decision made for me, with the threat of loss of employment, with no responsibility for the outcome on the people making that decision for me. I stated that, if someone makes a decision, they are responsible for the outcome, good or bad. I stated that the power to make the decision for ourselves had been taken away and that we were all being forced to be vaccinated upon the previously mentioned threat.

His answer, after three days of deliberation and consultation, was that we were all still able to make the decision … be vaccinated and employed or be unvaccinated and unemployed.

It was at that moment that I stopped working at the lab.

Oh, I showed up.

I got my vaccine shots like a good boy right at the end of the deadline by just a few hours.

I checked in and, only because of my conscience associated with my lifelong work ethic, I did everything that was required of me at work. But, I stopped being *helpful*.

And I started house hunting back home in The Midwest via the internet and a buyer's agent in the area I'd known since the seventh grade.

I moved my investments into short term mode.

I played the market in short, 2 or 3 week plays that netted extreme returns.

I poured more time and money into growing my side gig until it made enough money to cover expenses in a midwestern economy without having a job.

May had passed without me walking out, so I guess management thought they had made it through the whole 'I'm retiring in May' crisis.

They were wrong.

I had simply moved the timeline and deleted the part of the plan where I made sure they were taken care of and that all of my files were open to them and that all of my projects had complete turnover to someone else to minimize the negative impact of me leaving …

During the period from late Spring to late December, I showed up, did exactly what I was told and nothing more, and deleted any and all evidence of any work I had done or was in the process of doing on all of my projects. I got the damn vaccine shots. The first made me sick. The second made me even more sick. But I wasn't done with what I needed to do to position Sam and I for a comfortable, protected and well-financed retreat from the world of research and the East Coast economy.

I think that, somewhere along the line, they caught on. I never went back down the hill to where my old office was unless I was specifically assigned to do something in that building or if I had to use the counting equipment for radiological samples. Whenever possible I used the equipment at the radiopharmaceutical production facility where nearly every one of my colleagues in radiological physics were terrified and angry and not in a position to leave the lab … I was their hero by all accounts for my plans to leave. I didn't even tell *them* exactly when I planned to go. Just that I was going.

At least one of them was less of a fan than they led the rest to believe.

My daily assignment began to lean toward the mundane. Things that would normally be considered beneath assigning to 'the golden boy' and a waste of my scientific talents.

I continued to do exactly what I was told.

Then the assignments took a turn for the dangerous. I was sent into areas that were downright dangerous to my health and well-being. I was sent into one building complex that was so riddled with black mold that it was literally dripping from the exposed rafters and eating through the floorboards. When I reported the dangerous condition, I was told I should probably open some windows to let the place air out.

I got sick from that exposure. I was sent to the onsite medical center and diagnosed with a mold allergy and told to come back in a week for a follow-up panel of tests.

When I reported back to the OMC I was told it was just regular allergies and not to worry about it.

When I next made an effort to return to the building complex in question, it had been plastered with warning placards on the doors and windows ... No Entry Allowed Without Permission From Industrial Hygiene And Proper PPE To Include Respiratory Protection and Protective Clothing ... They later tore the building down and pushed it all into a big hole they dug ... at this time there is no record of the building ever having existed on the site map. But archival records in hard copy show it. And all of the documents generated due to my work in that building along with any correspondence associated with the discovery of the black mold and any electronic record of any associated conversations ... gone.

I wrote about it all as it occurred in my logbook, an official bound log that everyone in my department was required to keep. When I announced my 'retirement' with zero days' notice, my logbook was confiscated ...

Yah … In late December, we found a house back home via our buyers' agent. A cash offer was made after a walkthrough via Facetime on a cellphone and tablet PC. It was accepted. Closing was executed by my lawyer who resided in a nearby town back home.

As soon as that was done, I waltzed into the lab on a Monday morning and announced my retirement …

"That's awesome. When are you planning to retire?"

"Now … I'm retiring now … today."

"Hang around for long enough for us to plan a retirement party … a dinner … something like that."
It was phrased like an order … Like it was how it was going to be …

"Today."

"You can't … I mean there are protocols … paperwork … you have to turn over all your in progress work to someone and get them up to speed … non-disclosure documents to sign … exit interviews have to be conducted … I mean … it could take weeks … months even."

"Today … I'm done … I retire today. I'll come back in tomorrow to sign paperwork and sit through some exit interviews. Then I'll get my retirement badge and just pop back in when needed to close out anything else that comes up. If mentoring is necessary, you can pay me to do it as an independent consultant after the fact. Bottom line, I'm retired, effective now."

On Tuesday, I signed piles of paperwork and attended a few meetings, spending the rest of the shift popping into and out of offices across the lab property, saying my goodbyes and exchanging best wishes. Without exception I was met with smiles and well-wishes and genuine happiness ... Many treated the situation like the long overdue release of a fellow prisoner ... glad to see someone get out without dying or going insane ... Not long before Christmas, CJ had shot his wife then turned the gun on himself and not a single person who knew him had an inkling of why ... It was mentioned that it was good to leave before 'something like that happened to me' ... I wasn't sure how to interpret that, but it came from a smiling face and the concern in their eyes looked authentic.

The whole CJ situation/incident was yet another of the million straws that broke the proverbial camel's back. He was a young, new father, married happily, well-spoken black man with an awesome job. He was regularly trusted with greater and greater responsibility and was well compensated for it each time the scope of his job expanded. He was even appointed the head of the Diversity and Inclusion Committee about six months prior to his untimely and bizarre demise. No living witnesses. The child was barely six months old, so nothing could be found out through that method of inquiry. The wife was shot first, fatally. Reports said CJ the turned the gun on himself.

An odd aside … They said he shot his wife in the neck … That makes absolutely no sense. Along with that, I knew CJ very well and we spoke at length regularly about life and matters of a very personal nature and there was nothing in his life that did anything but bring him joy. Also … he didn't own any guns. We had a long conversation about high powered airguns that were all the rage among a new sect of hunters who used them for large game hunting. He thought maybe he could handle having one of those in his house since it didn't use gun powder and there was no real explosion and he wouldn't have to keep potentially explosive ammunition around the house for an air powered rifle.

None of it made any sense. And regardless of the sudden and strange circumstances, there was absolutely no mention of the incident on the news.

CJ … Nick … Townsend … Bill Z … The names and faces of the recently dead swam behind my eyes far too often when I was inside the protective fence that surrounded the lab where we had all worked together … In the time I'd been employed at the lab, I'd had far too many friends and colleagues meet untimely ends. It seemed no one died of old age anymore in that place …

Wednesday was pretty much the same deal … Paperwork all morning, then I made the rounds and said more goodbyes until about 3 pm when my cell phone rang.

"Pop over to building 400. They need your badge and then they'll issue your retirement badge. Might as well get it over with now while there's no line."

So I did.

But it didn't go like that.

When I turned in my badge, I didn't get one in return. It was a trick. Once they had my badge in hand, they said my retirement paperwork hadn't been processed yet and that they needed a section in it to approve issuance of my retirement badge. I was told to come back on Thursday to pick it up. Then … like Columbo used to do at the end of the show when he suddenly remembered something really important and sprung it on the unsuspecting bad guy … the badge lady came out from the back after having gone to answer a phone call …

"Sir … They're not letting retirees back on site at all during the COVID-19 reduced occupancy order … There's no sense in issuing you a retiree badge … They have orders at the gate not to let retirees in until the reduced occupancy order has been rescinded … Could be years sir … I'm sorry … And since you turned in your badge, we're not allowed to give it back to you … I don't know what else to tell you …"

She looked half sad and half afraid … Like she didn't want to be the one to deliver the death blow and she was told she had reason to fear me when she did.

I smiled and thanked her, then left.

A security vehicle with armed guards casually followed my vehicle to the lab exit.

I waved and made a right onto the William Floyd Parkway from the lab access road for the last time.

It was expected, in a way. While I was of use to them, I was the Golden Boy … so long as they were going to benefit from my continued support of projects, radiological logistics and experimental design. But, when I began to raise questions about the vaccine … When I went off site and had a discussion with that colleague … When I wrote that letter refusing the vaccine unless the people who had taken away my personal decision, took the responsibility that came along with it …

Let me tell you … I'm not the only one. There were others. Not just the vaccine issue. Issues in general with the way they did business … Supervision sleeping with direct reports then doing all they could to destroy that guy when the 'relationship' was over … Sending him to work at isotope production … under the supervision of her new boyfriend … That guy ended up on an FBI watch list, unemployed and living on the side of a mountain in New Hampshire … Everyone at the lab was directed to report any attempts he made to contact them … Anyone who received mail from him was expected to turn it over to supervision or security unopened … He was a really good friend of mine and I had to watch that happen … Anyone who didn't tow the proverbial line ended up in a very bad position. People who *never* touched alcohol being dismissed for showing up to the lab with whiskey on their breath … People in perfect health becoming suddenly, sometimes fatally ill … Murder/suicide by a guy who wouldn't allow a gun in his house … A high-level admin, tasked with looking into financial improprieties dropping off the radar for a week then being reported dead from COVID-19 … There were a ridiculous number of people with whom I either worked or associated closely, who were very careful about what they said or did at the lab … Some kept a copy of every email sent or received on a thumb drive 'as evidence' in case anything happened to them. Some kept two logbooks; one for management to see and one for what was really going on. The latter was kept in a locked file cabinet drawer.

I could go on for the next twenty pages about the nature of working at a government research lab and what it does to a lot of people. It requires a combination of iron-clad work ethic and a certain moral flexibility that does not come naturally to most people. You tend to be paid well and rewarded regularly when you perform as expected. If you do not, retribution is often swift and terrible.

I tried to retire in a graceful, responsible manner, telling them with plenty of advance notice that I would leave in May. It was made clear on so many occasions that they didn't want that to happen. For a lot of reasons, I ended up having to retire in the manner I did. It was against my normal morals and ethics, but it was unavoidable.

But, my manner of retirement from the lab and the methods I was forced to employ don't change the information I left with in my head and in countless thumb drives I've now had to lock away in a very remote location for safe keeping. It is my intention to leave them where they are in perpetuity, never to be seen again, unless they become ... necessary.

And, no ... I'm not the only one who knows where they are. No one near me knows. No one with whom I openly associate knows. But someone knows.

I don't think I need to write anything more about that.

What should the reader glean from all I have written here?

COVID-19 is real.

It is not as massive a threat as you've been led to believe, so long as you don't already have comorbidity issues that could be exacerbated by the virus. Treat it as you would a bad strain of the Flu. Wash your hands. Practice good hygiene. Eat healthy foods as often as practical and drink water. Exercise and be mindful of your general health. These are all things you should have been doing all along anyway.

Seven of the eight strains/variants of the virus would most likely not exist if we had just left it alone and let it run its course.

I know that's a terrible thing to say. People died. People we loved died. Lives were destroyed. Relationships ended.

But it would have been *over with* over a year ago if we had not coaxed into existence the other seven strains with a vaccine *that never was a vaccine.*

A vaccine, by definition, before they *changed* the definition, is a measure that, when administered to the patient, makes them no longer susceptible to the illness for which they've been vaccinated.

First, they said that if you got the vaccine, you would be protected against infection.

That turned out to be bullshit.

So, *then* they said that if you were vaccinated and got the virus anyway, you wouldn't die from it.

Fully vaccinated people were dying in droves.

So, then they said that if you were vaccinated and you became infected anyway, it would greatly reduce the severity of your symptoms.

There is absolutely no proof of that. 75% of people who contract COVID-19 or any of the variants thereof, show either mild symptoms or no symptoms at all.

By the time they got done lying through their teeth about it all, they had disqualified their vaccine as a vaccine.

It was *never* a vaccine.

It was, at best, a virus irritant that bred mutations in the virus that made it stronger and more resistant to treatment.

Your best defense is just being in as good of health as you can. That goes for any illness for that matter.

Masks ...

Look … They don't protect *you* from *anything* when you wear them. They do however prevent the open flight of liquid droplets leaving *your* mouth and nose from travelling as far and infecting others if you are indeed infected and contagious at the moment.

Boosters?

Make up your own mind about that. If you already have contracted and survived a COVID variant, odds are you'd survive it again with even less symptomatic expression that the first time. Again, that is so long as you have not developed comorbidity issues in the interim between infections.

COVID is the real deal, but it wasn't a potential extinction event. It was a natural culling of the proverbial herd from a purely scientific bent. From a completely emotionless perspective, it is an event that occurs on some periodicity to our species and has been occurring at said periodicity for eons and has continued to solicit the growth and improvement of our genome during our continuing evolution. An illness or environmental upheaval comes along and we adapt as a species and grow stronger as an end result each time.

Yah.

I know.

'You unfeeling, morbid bastard' …

Think what you want. Science doesn't give a shit how we *feel*. It has no consciousness, so stop anthropomorphizing 'nature'. And stop thinking that because something is terrible that it will end if enough people point out its terribleness … Not sure that's even a word. It won't. It will stop when it's done.

'Will COVID ever go away?"

No.

It's a part of the Corona Virus family and it has been around for as long as we can reach back and look for evidence of its existence and it will always be around, in some form or another, as long as there are living hosts in which it can grow.

The good news is, eventually, if we stop screwing with it, it will mutate less often and our natural immunity should be able to keep up with it. People will continue to die from it, just as they always have from colds and flu when they are severe enough to cause a fatal outcome.

What we need to understand is that COVID-19 is nothing new, in so much as *something* of its kind has been around at least as long as our species has been around.

And we evolved in an environment that demanded our genetic improvement and adaptation to an ever-changing dynamic in order to survive.

The genes that exist today are the product of millions of years of this ongoing process.

STOP thinking that a negative COVID test provides any protection. You could be infected ten seconds after you administer the test.

STOP thinking that the 'vaccine' provides you with protection such that you can wade into a crowd of infected people and emerge unscathed ... *because it's not a vaccine*.

In closing, the vaccine is a personal choice. It shouldn't be the basis for judgement or fodder for conflict. It shouldn't cost anyone their job.

It's not the magic bullet that's gonna save us all. And it damn sure shouldn't be the wedge that drives us apart.

It's not even a vaccine.

*Footnote:
For reasons of avoiding potential legal issues that could arise due to the publication of this book, just consider it a "work of fiction". I already have to spend way too much of my time looking over my shoulder. Don't make it any worse than it already is.

www.ingramcontent.com/pod-product-compliance
Lightning Source LLC
Chambersburg PA
CBHW051702250726
48653CB00007B/2796